To chipmunks Lily and Ollie for their inspiration,
and for John, Kyle, Lauren, Carly and Gill.

Copyright © 2016 by Caroline Carroll

All rights reserved

ISBN number: 978-0-9976695-5-8

Garden Box Press - Cape Elizabeth, Maine

Printed and bound in Canada

www.chipmunksinthegarden.com

Chipmunks IN THE Garden

by Caroline Carroll

Crocus

PURPLE WHITE

Spring

Viola

PURPLE YELLOW

Spring ❧ Summer

Tulips

ORANGE

Spring

Allium

PURPLE

Spring

Pansies

PINK YELLOW
WHITE

Spring 🌿 Summer

Peonies

PINK

Grape Hyacinth

BLUE

Spring

Hosta
GREEN

Sedum
PINK

Spring ❧ Summer
Autumn

Gerbera Daisies

PINK

Summer

Cosmos

PURPLE PINK RED

Summer ❧ Autumn

Daisies

WHITE

Summer

Geranium

RED PINK

Spring ❧ Summer Autumn

Verbena

RED

Summer

Gazania

PINK ORANGE
YELLOW WHITE
STRIPED

Summer

Zinnia

ORANGE YELLOW

Summer

Sunflower

ORANGE

Summer ❧ Autumn

Chrysanthemums

PINK **YELLOW**
WHITE **CRIMSON**

Summer ❧ Autumn

Pumpkins

ORANGE

Autumn

What Colors Do You See?

What Flowers?

Illustrations

The illustrations in this book are photomontages created by the author using photographs of flowers grown in her flower pots and small gardens in southern Maine. (One flower was photographed in a public garden.) Each hand-cut, layered design is an illustration rather than an exact replica of nature.

The chipmunks in the illustrations were photographed over several years while visiting the author's yard to forage for food and gather sunflower seeds. Photographing them at the exact moment they stopped moving was a constant challenge.

Chipmunks

Chipmunks are small mammals native to North America.
Distinctive stripes on their backs make them easy to identify.
Chipmunks forage, or search for food. They eat seeds, nuts, fruit,
grass, tender parts of plants, fungi, insects and even worms!
Sunflower seeds are a favorite food. Place a pile of sunflower seeds
at the base of a tree, or near a flower pot, and a chipmunk may visit!

Chipmunks have cheek pouches that enable them to carry food
for snacking or to store for later. Eastern chipmunks, active from
spring into fall, spend the cold winter months snug and warm in
underground burrows with the food supply they gathered and
stored several months prior to winter.

In your neighborhood you may see a chipmunk perch on a rock
wall, jump into a flower pot, run around in a flower garden,
climb a tree, or even chase another chipmunk. When chipmunks
try to climb flowers with long stems, such as tulips or daisies,
the stem usually bends or breaks and they fall off.
Chipmunks are always busy and fun to watch.

Chipmunks In the GARDEN
by Caroline Carroll